How Things Are

Poems by
James Richardson

Carnegie Mellon University Press
Pittsburgh 2000

Acknowledgments

Grateful acknowledgment is made to the editors of the following magazines, in which these poems first appeared:

Boulevard: "Defense." *The Formalist*: "In the Wind." *Georgia Review*: "A Disquisition upon the Soul." *Kelsey Review*: "For the Squirrels." *The New Criterion*: "Holes." *Paris Review*: "In Deer Country." *Ploughshares*: "Mothy Ode." *Press*: "Poison," "What It Comes To." *Princeton Library Chronicle*: "Milkweed, among Other Things." *Quarterly Review of Literature Poetry Series*: "A Suite for Lucretians" (a version of "How Things Are"). *Science News*: "For we have never, strangely, been within ourselves" (from "How Things Are"). *US 1 Worksheets*: "My Young Carpenter," "Nine Oaks," "'When Winter Snows upon Thy Golden Hairs.'" *Yale Review*: the poems of section II, "Under Water."

Thanks to the noble volunteers who read this manuscript and said what could be said: Julie Agoos, Paul Muldoon, David Orr, Chase Twichell, Theodore and Renée Weiss, and C. K. Williams.

This collection was completed with the assistance of a 1993–1994 Artists Fellowship from the New Jersey State Council on the Arts.

Contents

This book is for Catherine Richardson

I HOW THINGS ARE

How Things Are: A Suite for Lucretians

The new molecular philosophy shows astronomical
interspaces betwixt atom and atom, shows that the
world is all outside; it has no inside.

—Emerson

for Ted Weiss, that old Lucretian

1

Because the oysters I sucked down
were swished with Red Tide,
the fleeing of the stars
shifts red tonight.

Running a red
with the radio loud
or singing under a green,
even my brain's less mine—

Ah, Long Island wine,
and my new taste in ties!
Like you, I've seen what no one else has seen.
The universe will die before I die.

2

So it is spring, the season, as Lucretius says,
of Desire, skill of the world. Alas, so hurtfully young,
rumple of sheets still faintly on her cheeks,
she wanders, flushed, one button half out,
like a tongue just touching the back of the teeth,
or tangles on the floodplain's picnic blankets

in tableaus the iconographer would call
Venus enveloping hardbody Mars,
sleepily appeased, Love sapping War.

I like the other allegories better:
ice binding fire; or form and matter;
or sympathy and . . . whatever keeps us at our ourselves
when we are licked at, lapped at by desire.
The sand is swept downstream in toughening waters,
the breeze grows keen with smoke, the evening dense
with lovers its half-closed eyes have blurred together.
Listen up. And I will disclose to you the laws of heaven.

3

If there were no such thing as empty space, Lucretius says,
no atom could move, no new thought enter this universe:
there is no fecundity without emptiness.
Yet nothing can come of nothing without seed or cause.
Otherwise bluebirds, shaking off dust,
would hatch from the harrowed fields, and cattle,
lowing, amble from the storm-green sky.
All things randomly would greet and deny us, feed and fail us,
and creatures would flood rockwaste and woods indifferently,
gnashing at leaf and stone and nothing at all,
mistaking hunger for their food, and for their joy, austerity and
          pain,
but none of this can be imagined.

Men would stride out of the river, memoryless.
They would imagine themselves immortal,
and ride the trains bird-eyed, imploring, homicidal.
They might mistake love for a deadly thing
and batter children to save themselves from pity,
or shoot from a rooftop a crone swaying behind a laundry cart
as you might practice your deadly topspin serve.
But none of this can be imagined.

4

Between the Millstone River, just downstream
from the Sewer Authority,
and the Delaware and Raritan Canal
(disused) which two warm days
turn much too green

is a towpath, where you might surprise
a tangle of bikes
or a carp some laid-off fisherman, aghast
at its sheer albino size,

has left to a mannerly crow
that lifts, as from gift wrap,
quivering scarves,
rose-dust, and smoky blue, and mauve,

or the pink-eyed
guy with skinzines,

or me with my roar of a walk
and Walkman, head wide
with ten-in-a-chain moon-glossy
(oops I've been singing)
junk mail songs

O reader, dear!
(You have already won)
Never, O never before
(Our sympathy . . .)

Water, water, everywhere. . .
Though it probably wouldn't kill me.

5

For if each thing did not have its essence and seed
nothing would prevent a single tree from bearing
all fruits ridiculously, or each in its season,
and the mind would be lost in every image crossing it.
Parents would shudder and revert to infancy,
old men, mouths softening, turn into women.
Just by closing your eyes, you could distinguish the planets
by taste (those rocky herbs, red and green and blue),
or six pistons superheated, or each friend's failure,
but none of this can be imagined.

You would thrill with the narrow wind of the beast's desire,
glass wind of the stone's.
You would know how the deer's mind, leaping,
tones like the air in a flute, silver
and sudden as the long lake glimpsed through trees.
You would know through desire how to become anything,
as the lake holds any cloud, each sad migration,
each wooden bottom, each suddenly outcast line
it seems to itself to conceive of.

6

Because my immunity was compromised
I was invaded by living particles,
because I stepped ankle-deep through the ice
I was cirrus, keen across the moon,

because of stress,
because I scorned two aspirin and bed rest,
resigned myself to the poverty of pure relation,
neglected my office, hardly propitiated
Fever, the rock-bound Titan,
or because,

I have every disease.
I have heart shutting down.
I have noon, my brow hot lily.
I have evening's
repeating crickets, metastatic.
I have the bulls-eye rashness.
I have the undone.
I have August, terminally.
I have sleeping on an open magazine.
I have white, chronic dawns.

7

Nothing we know, Lucretius says, is nothing:
the unseen wind, he reminds us, must be bodies
small and soft enough to stir single hairs on your wrist
or find places on your skin so secret and grateful
you cannot tell the feeling of them from your feelings.
Yet surely they have hardness and strength in concert,
since they can herd a bank of clouds sky-long without
    derangement,
erect from the sea eighty-foot walls, or slide a ship
with the flat patience of continental drift,
just as rivers whisk houses from their foundations,
or wear canyons so slowly it hurts to think of the slowness,
even though water seems the softest thing to us
because we are water, and touch ourselves, touching it.

Similarly, downwind of a burning house,
you smell the fire-tang and your eyes water
though you saw no odors approaching, their ambush
so sudden, so much like remembering,
you have to remind yourself they are not everywhere.
No, they're a lake you can wade into, or walk out of:
as in the car I hold myself in the wind,
with your swift, O too swift, silence next to me,

and smell lilac for a mile, then henhouse,
diesel, mildew, laundry and what else,
as if a book went by too fast to understand,
or a runner's ripe heat, running just behind her.

8

Nothing is easier than that you assume me,
though if I squeezed next to you on the bus, smelling of wool
    and rain,
we might smile tightly and never look to the side.

You would not want to overhear my bitter prayer,
my thought of your perfume, least of all your name.
Like you I walked with my family and was helpless love.
Like you I wished for their destruction, not knowing I was
    wishing.
Like you I was granted perfections and did not feel them
    undeserved.
Like you I dreamed of making love to myself,
wondered if anyone saw exactly the blue I see,
knew no one was moved as I was by that love that song that
    season
and no one was bored as I was by that love, song, season,
knew you as myself, and did not know myself.

This entire warm front was breathed last week in Omaha,
rebreathed in Cleveland, and already
see how these long sentences lie down in you, knowing,
is it, or already known? You cannot stop hearing them,
though I am modest, I am polite. How is it possible
to be alone, since someone is always speaking
in the head, someone is always reading,
with a chancy candle, the middle of a sentence
that begins and ends in darkness.

Here, I am long gone
from behind these words, yet you hear them talking,
as the gull's cry seems to be coming from far behind the gull.

9

Nothing is just *out there*, Lucretius says;
its particles must enter us to be known.
Smell, for example, is the lounging of inhalations
along receptors complementary in form,
like fingers spreading for a difficult chord,
or the whole sky sliding soundlessly to dock
in the fine-toothed harbors of a fern.

That softly-repeated *plinking* on a jar,
distant at first? Listen more closely:
the rain's tower rises, and you walk,
steps echoing, in a huge cathedral
of hearing that has somehow entered you.
Hills left carelessly under the horizon
like someone sleeping, the sky, cloud-sifted sun
settle like fine gauze on our open faces
as if we were daisies, blind in the fall of pollen.

As for your slow extrusion from the ocean
failing colorlessly down your sides,
lift of your thighs against reluctance:
I *feel* it, I say, as if the eyes were hands,
for it is true, as desire tells us, that the world is touch,
or being touched—no telling the difference.
Always the shifting of tumblers, the whisper *Open*,
just as, moving against you at dawn, and lightly,
I am gray windows slowly lightening.

10

I can't get it through my head that the day is just in my head:
that I don't see *things*, only reflected light.
That I don't see light, actually, flitting between perches,
just the splash on my retina, the ripple
inward, of chemical potentials,
which isn't seeing at all—I mean, as I think of it.

It's as if I were watching behind video goggles
a movie of exactly the path I'm taking,
hearing on tape exactly what I hear,
though to God, looking down in trans-sensual knowledge,
it's darkness and silence we walk in,
the brightness and noise only in our heads,
which are the few lit windows in a darkened office tower.

11

But Lucretius, who does not believe in light,
not really, says that we see because things broadcast
images of themselves, continuous, that are material.
That jogger is shedding skins of herself like frames of a film
entering my eyes. The revolutions of the moon send down
husks of a moon, tree calls endless *treeeee* into the wind.
So the moon is itself a wind, the tree is a wind of seeing,
and the rose throws *rose* and *rose* down your welling eyes.

Naturally, the air is crowded with these films.
Your image, for example, and a wayward *horse*
superimposing, *centaur* might come to mind, though faintly
since such a thing never was. Imagination, we call it,
or dream, because these simulacra are so fine
they can enter through the skin, asleep, or any opening.
So, too, when *rose* and *moon* and *jogger* blend like winds:
I feel running in the skies, and a thorn of breath,

a gust of sweat and roses passing,
a body of moon my hands of moon pass through.

Images of all that has ever happened, further,
and all who have ever been, alive or dead,
persist in every place, at any time.
I concentrate, and your paleness rises through the throng
of clamoring shades. I.e., I remember you.
For the air itself is memory, everything's stored there:
faces we seek and recognize, all those strangers
who populate our dreams, or rise to become the faces
in books we read. It is all the air on our faces.

This is why no one asks you for your secrets.
Your whispers of love and shame in apparent privacy
are already heard, but so faintly who can be sure
whether it's you, imagination or the air,
in this life or the last, that whispers in them?
Now, as my past grows longer, things I did
in my faint youth are fainter than someone else's,
and things I have dreamed of, over and over,
stories I've read, lives scented on the wind
or distantly adored, history, imagination,
are strong as what was mine. I call them true. I call them truer.

12

The sun is bright because its images dive steeply
into our eyes, ninety million miles.
The breeze they drive before them
is how distance, Lucretius says,

is sensed in the eyes. Can you feel this
when you open to my gaze:
how the eyes themselves are wind,
wind with a question's rising intonation?

13

This is how it goes: all you are saying
expands in a sphere, an organized explosion,
though blurring, with distance, into wordless intonation,
until its vagueness, at last encompassing everything,
becomes unhearable motions, displacement of a pane,
rocking of airborne particles, faint heat in the walls
that not even a god's hearing can turn back into words.
Nor can you take them back, no more than remove
the blush from a cheek, these your root
in the world, your touch of everything again.

There is no standing that is not sending everywhere,
no waiting that does not rush out at lightspeed.
Even the un-happened, the never-told,
for these gave form to all you did, are raying out
to shape the future, though impossible, though unheard,
as my call ringing and ringing in your room,
and ceasing, leaves the silence ringing.

14

Dust of singer on singer, bird on bird,
dust of their images, broadcast,
dust of their songs that settles
on monitors and end tables

and in me, residuals of wind,
so I must be seen again, to grow light
after much fatness of seeing,
must speak, not to drown in hearing.

15

If everything is touch, then what's this soft
devouring of your drifts and drives, this blowing
through your tops and outlooks, under your shuddering doors,
this smoothing you like a map, or folding you small
to fit you into all these stories
I have to tell, this feeling you fit me into yours,
this saying O you *this*?

If I am the trillion fingertips of air
you form beneath, if we are waters blended,
perfumes unstoppered, gone and everywhere,
have I reached you, do I grasp you?
If I stand in you, my eyes behind your eyes,
if I underlie your breathing, rising where you rise
and cleaving where you cleave? Is it knowing

at all, this saying
that tries to be like seeing, this seeing trying to be heard,
these sentences, which are one further sense,
straining to vanish into something they call *you*,
or to be vanished *into*, as a lake makes
so much of its forgetting of the rain?

16

And if, as I dream, I touched you microscopically
as smoke touches air, if I entered you
at the level of the molecule, your carbon chains
stretching like power lines into a starless sky,

it would be dark, for there are no eyes on this scale,
and there's nothing to see, anyway, no face of yours
in no beneficent sky, no windy soul,
no signatory flourish of your limbs,

just atoms, like invisible constellations,
and light waves, propagating past me darkly,
as if I stood blind and deaf, even my thoughts turned off,
on the shaken platform of the Express.

This inside I've imagined would be an outside,
this merger I've desired, a further distance,
lucid, stellar, cold. O you *you*
who are a galaxy that has never heard of you,
as words have never heard of a beautiful line
or the beautiful line of its explanation.

17

Thus for our lightly, fluently repeated
wish to be light or wind or water—to be pure *move*
and blend as movements—wind and light and wind—
and no more rage at our massiveness and boredom,
that not-wanting-to-be-loved
undoing all our dreams of who we were,
wind in light and cloud in light in wind.

But then: the pillar taller than my body, the slammed door,
the light on the sill, the cliff between two notes,
the shelf booked-up in size-order, even the oft-sung pear
that reminds us, as everything else does, of the body,
and yes, even its truly boring
and sad oft-sungness,
and a tire's hot squeal, letting go,
are desire, and difficult, and difficult desire.
Why should I not have a garage,
a swabbed counter, a geode,
why should I not have a dog for a heart?

18

Why touch me, anyway, if *nearness* is just a metaphor
that leaves us in the cold? But to feel what planets feel,
holding each other to their swift ellipses,
their swinging out a form of their falling in: speak

around me, then, let me misunderstand
deeply, fail to compare yourself to me,
smiling stubbornly. Rise so steeply
I can clamber up, scatter my equipment,
sleep, and wake to mountains of the dawn.

19

For we have never, strangely, been within ourselves.
Never have I sailed the red arterial grotto
to my thick hand, have never and never
seen the mauve noon there, like the sun through squeezed lids.
I imagine the air mid-palm as dense and tropical,
but there is no air; breathing there is sub-marine,
continuous but hidden, molecular like time,
and, like time, runs without our willing

as even our will does. I say *I will walk*, but given the power
over walking, I would fall debating which nerves to fire,
which of a score of muscles to contract in order.
If I were responsible for everything in my body,
I would pass out from mismanagement of glands,
I don't even know the names of. As for the legions
of mitochondria and ion channels, how would I supervise them,
and still remember to draw breath in, to beat my heart,
as if I were charged with counting *a million, a million and one*
in a million voices simultaneously?

The body is what is done for us. From it
our dream of the world's beneficence derives,
from it, too, our helplessness, since, floating above it,
we do not know what we do or how we do it.
Thus our intensest pleasures, alone or together,
are pleasures, too, because they lose us in our bodies
with a slow perfection. I taste and fail,

or let music sway me with the wide slowness
of a plucked string in strobe. *It is rich to die*, I say,
torrents of darkness filling my closed eyes.
Old metaphor, but true, since it is true in dying,
whether from gunshot, heart attack, or cancer,
the last thing is: cells starve for oxygen and go down.
All deaths, in the end, are drownings in the body,
as what desire desires is drowning in desire.

20

Pretty convincing, what the brain's
original darkness, guessing what light was like,
came up with: eye.
As for the ear?
Ah, what it thought of air.

This plane in turbulence, dropping abruptly,
this one-more-stair-than-I-thought,
my foot sunk in the mole-soft lawn,
the wounded falling towards their wounds,
these swallows, hitting the sunset, gone,

must be what I've made of you: November,
white-blue and high
chamber in the catacomb
desire has hollowed, prisoner for life.

21

Come the thunderbolts, such is their suddenness
who knows whether they made us afraid, or our fear
or guilt summoned them, wrath of Zeus?
Thus when we hear what we least wanted to hear,
which means, of course, that we expected it somehow,
we say *It hit me like a thunderbolt.*

For the mind is not a point, as we sometimes think,
or the little theater where we sit alone, but many nations,
eye, ear, memory, knowing, knowing of knowing,
each in contact with the others by Long Distance,
and there's no one Place that is us, no single Present,
only the order in which we hear their calls.

So much that happens to us is ourselves, is timing.
A man who seemed to *think* of lightning, birds, a face
a millisecond before he knew he had *seen* them
might feel he was a god and had called them down,
or, take the milder case, might grow up feeling his power
because so much took place as he foresaw, or milder still,
might feel the world as a friendliness of happening.

Whereas the one who heard himself speaking words
a millisecond before he knew he'd chosen to say them
would find them like lightning. Would think
Even my own words happen to me.
I lie here, dead, listening for the voice of the god,
though even my listening is His Will in me,
as on the tip of a downbent branch, a dampish sparrow
opens its throat to admit a cry.

22

Hawks, rockets, lightning are fast, but the mind
concludes these journeys almost before they are thought of.
To Sirius? A matter of milliseconds. Ah, but how
do the continents remember to keep drifting
at a rate that imperceptibly becomes an inch a year,
how does the frost with a week's pressure,
such delicate and terrific pressure from every side at once,
harden and brown a weed without breaking a single stamen,
or in fifty years turn a hair gray? Slow's the wonder.

So many phenomena it pleases us to think of
as beyond process or performance, help or hindrance—
the reassertion over scarred ground, for example,
of the weeds, or the congregation of the clouds—
because to think of them this way (which means not
to think of them) leaves something in us free
and the world wild and full of gifts, what we call *real*.
Slow's the wonder; slow's the relief. But even wonders
have their essences and seeds, and patiently grow from them,

for time also is particulate, as Lucretius tells us, atom by atom.
Thus your wedding ring, over decades, slims with wear,
and a plowblade down the sillion shines and dwindles
as a knife with sharpening silvers into the air.
Lanes blacken gradually with the passing of tires,
and the stone stair is worn in the middle as if sagging
with heavy feet, and when it rains the water courses there.

Even the legendary lightning, slowly seen,
is a man descending a ladder, stopping to look down,
starting again to descend. Even light,
scrupulously imagined, is gradual,
though when will you calm, when will you ever gaze
with the steady openness that would slow its radiation,
showing the smooth striving from streetlamp down to street
of the individual waves, over and over?

Ah, everything happens for cause, and gradually,
and nothing disappears at once, or totally:
this is the thing Lucretius seems to tells us
that we most wanted to be told. That time
is also touch, and can be touched again,
and always the *having been* leaves traces of its being,
as if it remembered and would never leave us alone.

Or that's what we believe, regardless, we who trek
to the stairs the poet's foot wore, or look out the windows,
strangely askew now, of our childhood homes,
or weep for pleasure in apartments of old pain,
or greet the traveler who once stopped to listen
to crickets in the field, where, rumor has it,
the lover of the goddess rained down, blasted,
though reason insists coincidence of place is nothing.

For the mind itself is suasions of erosion
if we could pay attention—but that is the point,
isn't it? No one notices, in all the backing and forthing,
how the beach re-contours. "Suddenly," it is changed,
something is gone you thought was a love forever,
something lifted you thought would be heavy forever.
In the novel the children grow up in a sentence
and a young man wakes up gray and over, and Lucretius
. . . but now—gods, make me slower!—I cannot remember

how it took forty-odd years to get here,
page whatever, a matter of inches from the beginning.
And if I can't re-live it, second by second,
feeling the constant assurance of faint time
like the slight burn of kite string paying out through two
        fingers—
as, alas, who can?—then it is not mine,
and there is no such thing as a life, and my next step
may thrust into blankness white as the end of a line

23

Though Zeno, with his arrow that must travel
half the distance to your heart, then half of what remains,
and half of that, and never arrives,
proves motion impossible, since how could the arrow
      remember
over the huge chasm between instants
that it should be moving? So I am always half-way
to half-way to understanding: that the present does not exist,
though once it must have, since . . . see
all I cannot move back to!

Or maybe it's that we do not live in the present,
which is the rock in the stream
that splits us as we flow around it.

24

And I'm still not sure everything isn't fire
      as Heraclitus says,
sunfire starfire steelfire,
      or, slow-thirsting, burning coolly,
rockfire lakefire;
      since all our senses perceive,
rosefire jayfire,
      since chestfire, all I feel, and eyefire,
since the mind, too,
      like the fire in the hearth, its faces,
fire and darkfire forming each other,
      since the mind,
like all things in the windfire
      tears and shifts,
since
      timefire

25

But all things have an essence, and a time, and take their time.
Otherwise, why could not Nature produce men of such power
they could traverse the ocean as if it were nothing more
than blue carpet, dampish on a humid morning,
and break off Andes like the heel of a loaf?
They might eat the planet clean, or replant it
with aluminum forest and weep at its ruin.
They might, in whimsy, channelize our Southern rivers,
leaving them straight and navigable—
what could be simpler or clearer?—
and if they were also scoured of life, silt-choked, flood-prone . . .
well, here is the law of the universe, first,
that everything we imagine is too simple for us,
and second that our desires, given their way,
are powerless to undo their own undoings.
For desire simplifies and forgets, and Lucretius reminds us
things are more easily taken apart than put back together.
How could we live in a world that abided our consent?
I think of you turned to mine, to me, to yours,
to someone else's, to what you wanted.
I think, don't you, of our grade school art class—
how we waited in line to pour in the sink our rinsings,
how all of our visions, finally mixed,
made, every week, the same brown disappointed waters?

26

For all things are made also of what resists them.
Otherwise each Atlantic wave, incoming,
might spread over the prairies like a sky, and never stopping,
meet the Pacific, or each single, barely perceptible
spore of a fern might suddenly unfold
over us a green map the size of the world.

The peach, in its seed-instant, already turns and turns
as if the opposing air were coded in its dream
of how roundly it will ripen against the sky:
the essence of things is foreknowledge of their limits,
as the mime's body shapes itself backwards from finger
to shoulder with the touch of a wall it will never touch.

Thus for imagination, thus for desire:
time is the enemy they deepen against,
though it alone denies the return of the dead
they ached for, and all those loves unhappening.
It alone saves us from subjugation to freedom, it alone
prevents the fruitless practice of perfection.
Otherwise all stories are equally true
and there is no success or failure, heroism or shame,
no love some other story won't undo.
Otherwise nothing is left to the imagination,
otherwise there is no otherwise.

II   UNDER WATER

1 The Flood

So even having heard the news, I stayed
by the bay window, page unturning,
as the water rose, as it was growing
unsuddenly out of the air, like evening,
wetless, exactly body temperature,
and with such slight adjustment, breathable,
that only my slowing hands showed it was there.

Like your *Listen!* as it branches up a stairwell,
or your voice at a question's end, it rose.
With a faint jangle of hangers, closets were emptied,
with a soft shuddering, the drawers,
and the walls subsiding and the lapse of doors
were an old song played back too slowly,
the *I* and *love* now moaning *youuu* and *ohhh*.

And I heard (because sound travels under water)
the dinner mutter of my neighbors,
untroubled, nothing about the water,
though there passed, from left to right across my window,
what must have been their furniture,
and to the glass loomed momentarily
and open-mouthed, one or the other of their daughters.

Swallows, without a wingbeat, pour through evening
slowly as floaters dimly behind my gaze,
the phone rings, ember-slow, and streetlamps,
slowly as dragged-on cigarettes, grow strong.
The luster of eyes is an hour rising or draining,
and lightning of revelation, when it comes,
is a hand passing slowly down my face.

A glass of daffodils (for spring is floodtime)
at these depths is a blowless yellow gale,
the piano, in a haze of keys, faint savor.
Reach of my arms for reachlessness,
bay of my gaze now lessening in blue,
and all I have called my body: held notes failing,
as if I were being remembered, but vaguely.

2 Little Bridge

Suffering and smoking on the little bridge
(*teen,* as I remind myself, means *misery*)
they look up, glaze, the two of them,
Cancel alert: slow herbivore,
their scorn of me too lazy to be scorn,
my pity of them unfair, and not quite pity.

They could be us, in Year Whatever.
Same bridge. Same evening,
gazing into the water where your face,
as you straightened up to go,
expanded downstream,
and now is Now.

        If it were not for time,
I could be walking, right here, through your body.
I could be you. If not for the heart,
that will not let anything be,
that will not let anything be gone.

3 Salvage

Ever since Sanitation skimmed from the Outer Harbor
that sole impala, pale
with a driftwood phosphorescence,
I have known they survive, those drowned lands.
So gradual the invasion of the ocean
that the herds could mix again with waters,
browse Sargasso, stream Gulf Stream,
till their hooves lost touch with those savannas,
and veering, they sailed

as tawny, carnal clouds over the dream
that finds me in my childhood home,
still smoking, wrongly married,
trying to read what will have been
on a page ablur with dream-water.
All night, dark whale of sky goes over,
and dully the sandy lion of the combers,
and the rivers, long birds gliding in.

4 Undersong

Because I heard, under your murmur,
river as *swerve*, and pondering
pondering, the waves;
because it would not cease,
tree the jay's cry *tree*, and in the leaves,
alluvial, the rain's plural;
because it goes on and on,
though going, gone, our whither-thou-
ghost of a chance. . . .

Say *leaves, leaving*, blending *lull* and *weave*,
as in *the leave of my hands over you.*
How they float intently and slowly
like a prayer in no direction
fill leave   save˙ fail
or repeating, repeating, trying not to forget
a very long number;
like words, so wide now and so *were*
that they will not say *no you are, no you are*

5 Letter from One of Many Worlds

As you knock, if it's even you, a thousand universes,
like the moths on the screen door, wildly diverge.
In most, nobody's home. In some, somebody
dawdles or hurries to the door, bemused or eager,
with thoughts like these, if he's me, if he hears.

Or else you do not knock and, turning, meet me
as a bus brakes noisily and sparrows panic
and I walk out of sunset from another story,
wide-eyed with the early dark, and with the wonder
that my arms are full of groceries, and that you know me.

And of these stories, millioning their ways,
and of the sparrows, reeling, we are every one,
and in each eye the glint of all the others.
It is said these branchings, infinite, are the god.
If so, a god so swift it cannot remember.

Which is why, fond stranger, only I could tell you
of that other life in which I love you even now,
how we slept in pine-wind in a cold arboreal land,
how the faint ache down your arm and your shy, bewildered
      pride,
were once for a child that, now, you have never had.

But since no two of us have come by the same ways,
not even love's first lovers would dare to whisper
What do you know, what do you really remember?
and we live, as thieves stick to their alibis,
this life of which nothing is an example.

6 River Sunset

The brazen or sun-blonde,
the melon river, catching in its bend
faint slur of sundown, or the spray,
blood-golden, of a swallow.
The water grayed and mauve, aqua water,
whelmings and rinsings of your hair and sides
and grounds and fruit bruise and perfume,
all the taste of you swept
in a long tongue downstream,

where the deer look up,
where whoever plunged from the little bridge,
where softly on the lawn
(and sharply you remembered)
your foot sank down,
where the fabulous deluge,
and the creatures, two by two, would prove
there is nothing anyone,
not even the gods, may unimagine . . .

Under the moody clouds, under the thunder
played back too slowly to be understood,
some story you could not get out of your head
of the poor one unsolaced—
blue willows, island of Shalott,
peril of mirror or abolished tower—
who enters the long-souled
touch of the river,

where the coroner's boy,
poling the shallows,
draws up, gowned in river grass,
whom the water dissembles

whatever they were,
as beautiful lost women,
their silks untoppled, their lips
(and barely, you imagine)
wet by fastidious tides . . .

7 Water Music

And then she said, as if we were walking on the ocean bottom,
though it was a damp, soft-shouldered, stony road
in fog dense and free as darkness, early autumn,
our voices fog-reflected, hollowed. And then she said,
when a hundred feet off in the fog, where there was nothing,
brakelights flowered, and an engine kicked hastily in,
and a deer flickered through the rose air and was gone.
She said *he* said: something about fires dying,
growing, the road not taken, moving along,
something about self-something I'd have blushed at in a book,
though, as three rising and twining columns of smoke,
freedom and love and endurance above the ruin,
her pain, the child's, his, thinning to near-falsetto,
it could have been heartbreaking in a song.
Those were the words it gave her: what could she do but sing?
And what was my role but the unreflecting friend,
who turns, arms wide, to the darkened audience,
with *O the pity*, as it is written, and *Cruel destiny!*
and sparing no hyperbole of gesture
to say: *Forgive the badness of translation.*
This, as you know well, is tragedy.
Be grateful for the embarrassing simplicity
that allows you to stay, for two hours, just who you are.
Words fail her; they are supposed to fail,
and failing, become the intuition of the wish
she cannot see now will be too easily granted:
to be us, who hear, still settling in our seats,
her song *O, this is nothing you have heard*
and her song-to-come It was an old, old story.
Shouldn't I sing this to her, shouldn't a curtain . . .

shouldn't the moon break through now, or a cry made strange
in the fog?
but it is art that is short, and this, this would be long,
and we had already scared off what was in the dark, and were
alone.

8 The Water As It Was

Which at the velocity
of divers from the Verrazano
might as well be concrete . . .
Say here in the ancient ocean momently grown hard
these square foundations,
these doors
swaying and shutting with the ebb and surge,
these atria
failing of sill and caller,
damage and rule,
say this is the house
built of all the stones I ever threw in the water.

9 The Dreaming-Back

You would be surprised what stays:
the turn in the stairs
with the little table, the age in your face
that finally turned you mine.

Like the instant of drowning, some say,
or (the obliquity of the world over)
the dead's helpless remembering
according to intensity,
no way to tell memory from dream.

All things granted, now,
why should they care for desire?
The most trivial sin they could not confess,
some uncalled-for explanation
never explained away,

refusals, sheer dull presences:
these, like heavy stamens, draw the beating ghosts
that yearn now to be balked,
only then bodied, only then living again.

10 The Bridge Again

There is a tweed coat swirling waterlogged,
and there a spar with a clinging rubber glove,
and small darknesses like opening mouths.
These are the satin waters that undress
softly and so many, spendthrift waters.

As to be blinded in the darkness of a stairwell,
or surprise in your reflection one you loved,
or lose in the day the day's unlikeliness,
here the all-foreseen runs swiftly never-done,
yet holds so firmly the image of the moon.

III   WHAT IT COMES TO

On My Roof

Nothing expects to be looked at from up here.
Who worries about their car-tops, their hat-tops?
My neighbor, sunning topless, never looks up.
Houses seen from a roof are roofs: black, tan, and slate
steppingstones across a treetop bay,
whale backs, maybe, under shaky plumes of steam.

Everything's as the crow flies. I can't see, under leaves,
my left on Snowden, right on Hamilton, but near
that tall antenna is the underwater school
where I dropped my busy-minded Kate for the day,
and, in an archive foundered off that Gothic spire,
Connie pores left to right, down, left to right,
through incunabula that history sails over.

No wonder they're known for flightiness—
roofers, I mean. Who visit and vanish like starlings,
leaving our bedrooms half exposed to the weather.
Only thirty feet up, Life?: a complete abstraction.
Contracts weaken as the square of altitude.
Family, memory also. I guess the absconded crews
wake in rowboats, with a snort, or scattered bars,
and only the scent on their hands, of roof tar,
guides them up ladders they must have sleepwalked down.

Pilots must feel this also, looking down
on the counties we pedestrians struggle through.
Penthouse dwellers, fire wardens in their towers,
surgeons above wet deserts of the body,
killers looking, small-eyed, down. Anyone looking down
from the mind, anyone looking out of eyes must feel it:
nothing but *but* separates us from what we desire,
but there's no way to get there, either.

Poison

The tulip indolently cool
left tilted in a glass just to say *This
is the thought I had of you,*

through no one's fault that I can tell,
unpetals, opening
one red door, then two

on Katie, who's knelt at toadstools,
beetles, three leaves glistening
with *Is this poison? Is this poison?*

ever since learning that our fungicide
has the same name, *bluestone,*
as the pebbles whose rich gnashing

means someone coming up the drive.
(Tell: is it the flaw,
desire—or the rule?)

Now in quest of *magic crystals,*
dangerous or true,
whose difference from ordinary gravel

(at least, as far as I can tell)
is in her wanting them, she glances up,
hoping to see no one at all,

because she's wandered almost far enough
to get called.

Alcohols

And what would a little guy be wanting with that, said Irish,
suspicious, and rightly, of my hands-in-pockets shyness,
till I described my lamp, clear glass, squat oval,
and maybe I added, or maybe he heard, *Mystic, alchemical,*
since he laughed that likely it'd burn forever
on my dollar and change of cool, denatured ethyl,
And careful, kid, not to knock it over . . .

It burned with a day-blue neither fire nor air, so subtle
only the cellar's darkness made it visible,
peopling my lab with a ripeness like bruised apples
and a TV's exhalation, hot, ozonal,
spirits that would not mix, or mix with mine.
As for my wish, it was ravishingly simple:

anything heated long enough, it was my child's surmise,
would break down: gas driven furiously off,
leaving the sheen of undressed metal.
Held to the flame, my crystals carbonized,
but if I was kidding myself about their glow—
lithium, silver, tantalum, or *iron*—
there was no one dying to tell me so.

That I'd stand in a fire-lake streaming ignited runners
(lamp overturned, or leakage suddenly catching),
that I'd shine one instant, massless with fear, looked-through,
that I'd burst upstairs to tell, that I'd leave untold
the world-undoing thought I had exposed:
what they say will happen, happens, as by now one knows.

Too cool to hurt me, touching nothing off . . .
I would meet someone with eyes that serenely

lit-from-behind blue. Who would say she loved me.
I would sip my gin, pausing, I would say no
and rise. Blue everywhere. Skies. Flames subsiding
into a basement bar, a stair, a door of rain.
It made sense, what the label warned, that drinking it would
    blind you.

Defense

And as for my errorless season in center:
from the bat's crack and the angle of reflection
I would gauge the resentment of the hit,
and where it would travel getting over it.

And though I was sprinting flat-out, or laid on the wind
in some bone-breaking dive, it was my study,
for one long moment, always to have been there
(*Range subsides to basin; summer, in your moody,*

deepening gaze, is Fall; a dream, years long,
happens within the sounding of an alarm.
How kind the night . . .) looking that moon of a ball
with still eyes into the stillness of my hands.

For even the boy who dreams of launching homers
through the outer planets, all contact lost,
saying to the face unmet *I will never need you,*
learns no drive is complete till it is caught.

Till his prayer falls stingless into the mind of god,
and touch, eyes closed, cannot be told from touched,
and in the listening darkness of the glove
it is no more blessèd to give than to receive.

My Young Carpenter

"I'm not a man of many words," he says *drack drong*
hammering. Though once, and oftener than once,
"Just married" *thwang* and "Now that I'm married . . ." *throng*.
And when he pauses to breathe, deeply, his hand,
how can my glance up, weeding, fail to comprehend
he is turning his young wife over in his mind:
as many entrances as a half-framed house.
How, in his conjugation, *drenk drank dronk*,
from sheer manyness her beauty is revolving
with duty *drack* and tenderness *tat tat*,
and blind guesses. How sometimes looking down at her:
slowly as darkness climbing to find soft stars,
he enters himself, finally deep, with a sound
like a sanding stroke, or a car's traversing *zwishhhhhh*.

Unlikely his hovering lightness, finishing *det dit*
what he builds for me, deft-jointed, and for himself,
him with no house yet, drawing plans—for a child,
is it? He's not a man of many words: they are
difficult as getting a huge bookcase around
a turn in a narrow hall, and irretrievable.
As for work: there is more time to get it right.
Here a door still doorless, stair still open-mouthed,
the walls so slowly closing out their closing in,
the roof, half weather, on which he is stapling down
tar paper, *pack-it pack-it*. Simple the works of men.

Holes

Since I've learned little by little
how these things go,
that a pond might be a field's

blue deepening
where it has understood the sky,
since maybe this explains my eyes

or how my body learned its hollows,
flute-long, from your embouchure,
since all these arguments are full of holes,

it's silly to scheme against my flaws
as if they were not mine,
as if they were more than one

window scissored open
in a snowflake, which a child's
unfolding multiplies:

gaps in my calculation,
knee suddenly air,
terrible weakness for the smell of your hair.

A Disquisition upon the Soul

It doesn't register the kid on rollerblades,
or two on the bench that wind sends lightly together,
or the *Times* they leave, or who sleeps under it.
No, those are the heart's. The soul is an old, slow camera
that shows which way the waveless ocean was,
and the day, and darkness, and again the day;
but all things moved or moving, us or ours,
it sees through. Therefore it does not see them.
Is it the restlessness, then, that in the thick of our lives
sends us to windows, wishing for the end
of all that has made us happy? That, sadly,
is also the heart. The soul would not know
which dying friend you thought you could leave for dead,
what shattering love you could leave your daughter for,
or that you stayed, since no one stays long enough;
and, being immortal, hardly knows it was alive
when it is back where it came from after all our years,
as faintly blued as snow is from the height of our skies
and heavier only by the sound of waters.

Three Inescapable Sentiments

for Kate at 5

1

Though they look a lot like ordinary gravel,
you're sure they are fossils
and read them to me.
This is a trilobite, this the print
of a tiny saurian toe—
and this, would I say this
is spider's networking,
a fern's lash, or the wing of a bee?
O, all of the above. And breath's
haze on mirror-stone. And hope
nothing shall disprove.

2

Shadows, whenever they get together
for a long night, or scheme behind a barn,
say it is they who cast the sun.
But when I thought I was dying,
I knelt by your bed, whispering to you,
sleepy, puzzled, and fond,
until your beautiful lashes came down,
to be yours as long as I could.

3

So there is the soul—it looks like me, as I knew it would,
turning with the quick wave I have learned must be enough,
since I did not cause my soul, nor may I keep it
from clambering up the bus steps in red snowpants
into what seems to be darkness, lost in excitement.

Nine Oaks

It hadn't seemed so bad from my study—
thronging gutters, struggle of windows, thunder—
but here, nine oaks that were a hall of calm
are hugely uprooted. More than a century,
surely, they had overarched this road
like guarantors of gravity. Now they show
how shallow the roots are that we teeter on,
how much higher, and still higher, the blue
it seems my little car might plummet into.

There are worse catastrophes, Lord knows,
I mutter, half-mad at my tears-on-cue.
Who but blissheads believes in the pain of trees?
(But who believes only what he believes?)
And maybe the rootcloud's helpless paleness
touches, where all losses are the same,
as one glass, rung, sets others thinly singing,
upon the paleness lovers love to find
that shouldn't be out here for every eye
and the damage of light going on and on.

Or maybe these trees, though not our property,
were something I had counted on to stay.
When I was younger, I wanted to hear sages
say everything grows again, to everything its season.
But less of life seems replaceable, now
when the less that's left seems somehow more my own.
Some things I will see again. Things that take time—
great trees, a nation's peace, or a friend's,
or on the white sill just that patient light—
may come back to this life, but not to mine.

What It Comes To

Now that my eyes are going,
all distances are tricky.
Fine print, for all I can guess,
says: what I'd like to have written.
I can't tell a jigging
white-tailed deer
from the flutter of old beech leaves
or a white-shirted somebody
who has stopped his car
and stumbled through woods
(so grayed and hazed
only reason says it's not a woody cloud)
to check if a glint he happened to descry
was what he hoped, or a tin roof,
a high window, or my softening eye.

"When Winter Snows upon Thy Golden Hairs"

Falls sparsely, vanishing mid-air, about Thanksgiving,
a phantom in your hair, less weight than brightness.
Brief flurries, December, meld with our black drive
as if it were water. A little stays on your coat a little while.
We wake, weeks later, to a dusting gone by noon,
and the first white hair in my chest—a pen's run dry—
which I pluck, and before I can show you, lose.
In the short run, time's a shoreline, losing and gaining,
or a mood, warmer or colder. Snow comes and goes.
For a day, a week, I might be as young as I choose.
But it comes and stays, storm falling on uncured storm.
If this is the Ice Age, it will stay all summer.
I shovel enough of a path to live, I shave,
but I'm counting on moderation now, I'm calling on spring.
It's more than a metaphor we have to survive.

In the Wind

I wanted to be the fold of water,
trout or wind at the surface,
unsure, so light and quick it was,
whether I'd seen, or heard it.

Thick as a tree stump, I would dream
I was leaves, in their morning-long
dawdling and lateral fall,
that a gust ran off with, slip of the tongue,

or see, in the blue of evening, blue
smoke swept sharply down,
a light dancer fleeing her partner,
all plosive gown.

When will I learn my part of love
is not to be blown away,
but to stop, as I do, and praise, as I have,
what winds I've gotten wind of?

IV INNER ANIMALS

Mothy Ode

One of those pizza-like images of the moons of Jupiter
before computer enhancement is how I look to this moth,
since that's how everything looks (see Monet, etcetera)
before the brain, with help from personal history,
cleans it up. And this moth, the poor trustee
of one small fraction of a thought, has got no room
in its two-byte brain for *This* or *Feed?* or *Breed!*
and *Clean it up* together. And as to history: *Huh?*

So I'm *Bulk, vertical*, joined firmly to the earth,
the same as a bookcase or a tree. This pleases me.
Does a moth see depth? I guess it would have to
to steer boldly among stems to find whatever it finds
(what do moths eat, anyway, nectar? air? ignorance?)

Its life must be a video driving game,
cartoon-like obstacles rising up, its own swerving
difficult to tell from the roads. It can't have room
for the thought *I'm steering* as it steers, giddily,
down the slope of pheromone concentrations
in something that feels like providential falling.
Something thinks *for* it, the moth would think, if it could
        think.

From a moth's angle, I am the sheer heft
of Otherness, in all its inexplicable wonder.
Everything about me is pure instress, startling me-ness,
my gaffes and hesitations wired from birth.
Even the frantic waving of my arms, Hey *Moth!*
seems to declare me a creature of pure nature,
though it looks to me like considerable calculation.

In tragic opposition, some Super-Moth might mourn,
the quality of Mothness is fixate on high contrast
and, surging again and again (in a kind of software crash)
into romantic candles, or unromantic porchlights,
roast and pulverize. Ah, this is beauty, all the soul can take
of passion's endless loop! Which is not so pleasing.

Whereas a human's amazingly fluid slowness (to a moth)
reveals a being unburdened by desire (like a stone
I would say, but moths don't notice stones) and wedded,
by a massiveness beyond conception, to the planet,
or, as their apostrophe to us goes,

Anchor,
wind-strayed never,
into no sun falling,
daystander, pure endurer
of the dazzling brilliance of our drives . . .

or something like that, and we who can sit so long,
looking at pages (it seems to them) of darkness,
we with the calm of oceans and things too slow to be visible,
we who are indistinguishable from each other,
how could we suffer reverses? Well may they whirr at my
          screens

Thou was not born for death, immortal human—
the bulk I see this passing night was seen
by ancient polyphemus, hawkmoth, luna . . .

in ultrasonic worship. Why *shouldn't* I,
since they ask so little, mime, as for my children,
a simplicity that might ease their faith?
The god-part comes so naturally: *O little ones!*
hear my thunderous speech, each word long as a moth-life.
The flame I look upon unmoved. Also the porchlight.

All that your flitteriness leaves ungrasped,
I hold up, practically an Assistant Planet.
I am the blindness with which the Universe

beholds itself and knows itself divine.
I am the huge unmoving root
of that body of which you, O jittery ones,
are the tips of the fingertips, and when I ponder
I grow perfect as darkness, disappearing. There.

For the Squirrels

These squirrels, they are like dishes or socks or magazines,
needing again and again to be put away,
or like asphalt and telephone poles, so ordinary

I shut some neural door on them. But who
loves you, O Squirrels!, who else intones *O, Squirrels!* to you
because of your really interesting boringness?—

though you won't stand still for apostrophes, probably eat them
along with insects, buds, the occasional nestling,
nuts legendarily, and anything portable

that does not eat you, except daffodils, toxic,
which nevertheless you officiously transplant
to bloom incongruously mid-lawn, mid-traffic island.

As well greet my lymphatic system or heating ducts
as friends, and to call us enemies, since I do not raise corn
or harvest nuts, is rhetorical overload. Ah, but lend

to my spacy drift your lifetime coffee nerves,
and effect cartoony violence in my attic! Be my exclamation,
so that, jazzed-up, squirrelly, I may grasp our relation!

From the Greek for "shadow-tail," from Indo-Something
    suquirt,
from *squirm,* from off-key *skirl,* a.k.a. *chickaree,*
fairydiddle, tree rat, even *oak cat,* squirrels begin

in selected mythologies as something like wired bears
whose visionary worries make them radiate mass
till they shrink to the size and jumpiness of a mind—

that they are hyperactive in light rain,
when everything sensible hides, confirms it:
they scarcely have bodies. Weather does not happen to them,

or calm, certainly not bullets, so the fabled Brunswick Stew
must be made with pork, tall tales, and the millions that have
        perished
of nervous overload from a near-miss.

Transparent to gravity, they beam vertically,
or traverse the power lines like a furry sine wave.
Yes, they are the fluffy incarnation of current,

stopping suddenly with an electrocuted tremor
(in quantum terms, a cloud of squirrel probability
condensing unpredictably into a single rodent),

and sometimes, luckily, a squirrel/anti-squirrel pair
spirals up a tree in a barber pole pattern,
virtually virtual. They must mate as leanly as clocks.

One of the four non-domestic mammals, six birds,
eleven weeds and no amphibians
to which the entire world (though none are native

to Antarctica, Australia, or Madagascar), a suburb of itself,
has been reduced, one of twenty words that have fastened on me
hopelessly (but don't me let me repeat myself

squirrellishly) and perfectly adapted for human margins,
        competitors
ebbing into the shy woods, their only predators cars...
or perhaps, after all, humans are adapted to squirrel margins,

our cities merely inefficient means of producing
plunderable feeders, poets with nutty odes to them,
and little children *Here, squirrel, here* with bread in their hands.

Milkweed, among Other Things

Suppose you found in an unlikely place,
by which I mean unlikeliest to you,
the most *beautiful* (I have to use the word)
the most beautiful thought you'd ever happened upon,
but arrived at no way you could understand,
and since no one had ever commended it,
and you had no means even to say it,
it was *without price*. Would you sell all you had,
would you, forsaking others . . . etcetera?

Consider the milkweed, among others,
found, by definition, in all the wrong places,
"waste fields, roadsides, disturbed ground"
(gardens are even wrong when it's around),
wherever suppleness, quick growth, and many seeds
can compete (i.e. where there are no trees).
Consider the weed? Weeds *have* been considered.
Discovered in their vivid overrunning
of a place that yesterday was nothing but place,
or flashing in the rear view like a lost chance,
or splitting the interstate with blue flowers that recall
what asphalt shortcuts massively repress,
they brace us with their unexpectedness.
Over and over, as the phrase goes, *there they are,*
reassuring in their mere persistence,
light, free of the past, helping us to believe
that the world will do just fine without our care,
which for one era, gentleman and ladies,
made them virtual symbols of *laissez faire,*
but let that pass. See "Poetry of the Eighties."

Consider the milkweed, coarse, and sillily tall,
and Dumbo-eared (even Frost, in a snit,
opined "For drab it is its fondest must admit"),
and dangerous uncooked, causing spasms,
profound depression, labored respiration,
"the symptoms," Crockett quips, "of a man in love,"
owing, perhaps, to the milky latex
from which the larval monarch borrows bitterness
in superstitious dread of gods above
(muddling along, both wit and vision blurred,
no caterpillar has seen the guessed-at bird).
But close up, as its lovers could attest,
(the generality of Frost's description
argues for change of distance, or prescription)
the milkweed, in its several thriving versions,
rose, orange, white or lavender (the best)
is—what I can't quite say. Two out. Ninth inning.
Didn't we talk about faith at the beginning?

Pushing a point, I could presume you, too,
have thought the floweret's pentagon, strict, cool,
when gathered dazzlingly in hive-like umbels
is something seen through a monarch's compound eye,
which, like the panes of a revolving door,
splits images four ways, sixteen, sixty four,
and sweeps you inside. Odorous vaults,
the suddenly-above-you workings of an ocean
so vast and lavender it might suggest
Heaven itself as thought by an amethyst.

But maybe not. And no one compels a vision.
Words are not things or halls. Still less, oceans.
They are the weeds waiting everywhere for you
to happen, or not, upon your own surprise,
to hear in their muteness, as you do, a voice,
and find your wisdom, as you will, unwise,

and sell all you have for the faith, unlosable anyway,
that somehow we can talk to each other,
which, though priceless, must be given freely,
since neither beauty nor *beauty* can be earned,
though found, as if by accident, together.

For the Birds

Where are the songs of Spring? Aye, where are they?

The one that says *soothe soothe* to the roofs,
the one that says *3-D 3-D*,
the one that says
(Thoreau says) *drop it drop it*,
the one that makes me look up
thinking it's the brakes of the mail truck.

*

Like a word I've given over
trying to remember, *Spring*.
To say *too soon* too late
or *too late* too soon.

*

One that leers, one that disparages,
the owl we have never seen,
the *skrawk* of drawer.

Is it the redwinged blackbird,
that vocal interbred with metals?

Somebody somebody
owes me a letter.

*

I forked up in half-frozen garden
body or fibrous tuber,
beak or seedhusk, was it?

Was it foot or root?
And smoothed it back as hopelessly
(quartz eye or eye?)
as when my teeth came out in hands
like words I could not take back,
or in the silver mirror, slivering,
my wan face fell in petals.

*

whose is the dawn song whose is the dawn
never remembered until heard
whose is the dawn

*

Why should it be important, this smattering of spokes
and snatch of song she passes me with
that, with huge earphones, she can't hear she's singing,
head back, *wah-Wah* and *Wah wah Wah?*
Haven't I known forever: interior is aria,
toes to the stage edge, darkened audience?—
song is not to be heard, song singing
No one is moved as I am by this song.
Why, if I've known forever, *Wah wah Wah*
wah Wah wah is my heart so bro-o-ken?

*

The quickening ping-pong ball
of *dit* and *dit*
and *dit dit dididit*

a bug? a bird   a bird? a bug (a bird)

*

A pot that has begun to stick,
lump in the throat,
last chink of night,
last rag of snow,
the blot where the printer jammed,
all letters at once—
O little dead thing
that patience will untie,

one thread of CO_2, a rope of sands,
cord of its song,
and miles-long strings of light and water.

*

Whip poor Will
wee-eep wee-eep
chuck Will's widow
why me? why me?

Thus folk imagination
hears narrative or lyric
(do or be done-to)
in anything *re-peated* and *re-peated*.

*

Another head wrapped in an unheard song,
nodding *one*, nodding *one*
like someone waiting for the bus to empty
to get on.

*

Children too elfin to stand still for love,
punctuation without words
(veer of intonation as the sentence ends?)

each an enormous
photon, the flock
only the quantum uncertainty
of one,

how we look to each other,
how I look to myself forgiven,

not saying *you you you*
to anything you come upon

*

Its wings-flat glide, or better,
its funny little flick,
nearing a branch, to land tight:

grace, I mean, its Indo-European root
of the same tender wood
as *gravity*, as *grief*, as *gratitude*.

*

the one that climbs from *peek* to *pique* to *peak*
the argument: *same same   free free*

*

three on a sing
three on a sing
singsong
(sang the singers,

quick stars blown dark
before they burnt God's fingers)

*

(As for the secret english on my English:
inaudible, I've learned, to anyone else:
let it go? What no one else can tell me
how can I stop whispering to myself?)

*

somewhere in the tuliptree
has been   will be   has been   will be

*

Is this the end   the end
one says
          one says
No this is   this is

In Deer Country

They return in desirable colors of the season,
whether casually or stupidly, to simplify the garden
of its sweetest shoots and tips, though I have set out
dogbane and stinking tansy in a rage,
nightshade and firethorn and bitter sprouts
and bepissed with the collusion of the moon
the glistening rows, so that half a county downwind
any pack of them, suddenly transparent
with hunger at a crossing, will feel as surely
as if they were in my heart that this is land
too poisonous and overwrought to feed upon.
Yet since no vigilance, since vigilance conceals them,
or darkness, since no dark is dark to them,
can hinder them, the flowerhead loosening,
the red-green leaflet oilily unfolding,
and my curse, found tender, will be gone by morning.
They will tide, like sleep itself, through the shaved beds
to nip the rusty mums and the frost-breathed asters
within a handsbreadth of the sighing house,
where I stood once to declare *I have lived forever*
on this hillside, with its gaze-deep cover
and the stream the deer do not bother to step over.
My woods, as I watch, will clear into a park,
the old trees growing older far apart,
though I mortgaged for them both desire and memory
when I thought time was my only enemy.

V THROUGH AUTUMN

Through Autumn

for Connie

1

On a wooded hillside, staring into woods,
our house is built on a punched-down bulge of fill.
If my eyes could bore through the trees and one more hill
I would see New Jersey's sandy and paler green
flat-out thirty-mile run to the sea—
though for kids like me, who grew up on plains
where the streets are loomed with wires, and the sky is a stare,
not to is the point of buying here.

2

A tortoise and wild turkeys (six),
a luna moth, a great horned owl,
two half-imaginary foxes
we save like passes to the next world.

3

Storms stumble on us, hurrying from the West,
as if there were one more step than they expected,
and in their thrashing fall take down century oaks
and the tops of soft-wooded tulip trees.

In an hour all the rain in town is here
via the doubled and redoubled tumbling stream,
or the conduit we hear licking under the drive,
or the sourceless outburst at the foot of the hill.

Our little glade, technically wetlands, softens,
and the sun pushes out, hammering the damp
into midges finer than any screen
we swab like ash from beneath a left-on lamp.

4

All night, the strange busyness of night,
something desperate wailing *Paul Paul*,
too monotone, we decide, to be a woman.
Mockernuts and acorns swishing down.
Morning, no change, nor any sign
of the paint can or corrugated tin
that one in ten, plummeting, rang like a gong.

5

The expectant trimness of the houses, a reserve
more revealing than confession:
like the perfumed mirror, the straightened dresser
of the room you blunder into, hoping
for your stashed coat when the party's over.

6

I could write a field guide, *Faint Hums of the World*,
distinguishing the subliminal calls
of thermostat and fritzed transformer
from Black Cable Box and Greater Electric Clock
for the benefit of panicky new homeowners
whose bodies are houses, now, whose hearing is larger.
I need to know, lights out, on my loud pillow,
whether it's choral digestion of the gypsy moths

or the cosmic background radiation I hear seething,
or the sound of my own, or of someone else's, listening.
(I pad downstairs to be sure it's nothing).

7

Too many starlings, too many deer
and squirrels. Our little stream
unslurred by algae, disturbingly clear,
supports nothing but waterstriders.
Hardly a toad or warbler, overplus
of honeysuckle, bluejays, lawn:
ecologically shallow, you might say,
the way the soul gets when too busy,
or insisting to itself *I'm happy, I'm happy.*

8

The *clock* of plate on plate,
aspirin's rattle,
the radio's intermittent
nerves of static,

button ticking
and ticking in the dryer,
unballing paper's
crackle, timid fire,

and the click bug—how
it got in, I don't know—
like someone's typing out,
unbearably slow,

of a list. But what is it a list of?

9

In the kitchen, somewhere, but we can't root out
the *inner cricket*, as we call him,
huge-sounding, probably speck-like,
precision almost electronic
in his timing of the year's pure running down.

10

You can hear them in the eaves
like a radio faintly receiving,
or a drink fizzing flatter,
the carpenter bees,
chewing their bullet-round holes:
blunt, black
and stingless, though their lumbering
can unsteady you on a ladder.

11

Blast from the quarry, groundwave first,
shockwave arriving out of step.
Between them all the disasters
I have to remind myself it isn't.

Not a siren: my wind-leaky car's
whistle, like a teapot starting.
Not the door, but a flicker
knocking at a maple gone soft-hearted.

Not the unburied Titans
fumbling in their pockets for loose change,
just the recycling truck, its pouring clash
of metal on metal, glass on glass.

Time after time, Nine Tones,
the gods' names in this age,
are arranged and rearranged.
In their true succession,

(trashcan rattling down the drive,
flicker knocking at the eaves)
something in the day will fling open,
our bodies blow off like leaves.

12

Or how about the carrion beetles,
black and yellow, and so like the panels
of the roadkill turtle they were feasting on,
that for a long minute, while I tasked and tasked
my eyes to stop seeing what they saw, I was sure
the parts were walking away from the whole's disaster?

13

The power bucks, then goes out.
We go by wide-eyed instinct through the house.
Here turn, step, duck, here turn again.
Roughness of wallpaper, dead switch,
the height of a riser, count before the landing,
everything invisible but memory,
firm under our feet, taking our hands.

14

Floor of the study, patch of warm?
Ceiling light on in the room downstairs.
Kitchen floor's wet chill?
Ice chip, melted. Or another of the dead
has walked out of the Great Water.

15

Turn in the stair: the smell
of dinner lingers, bubblegum,
mildew that in some breezeless corner
has resumed doubling.

Since that may be gas,
skip the matches, pass
the mirror darkly,
fearing the flick of a switch
for its tiny blue spark,

or the tiny yellow one
where the key slides into the cylinder
or your knuckle cracks, or one thought
sets off another.

16

Even the phone ringing
like the long release of rain
when a tree's blown, long after rain,

even the VCR, its bright addition
of 12 and 12 and 12,
even the spreading blue

the pen I fell asleep on shot me with,
even the tick of a downspout, like a heart
forgetting to ask why it keeps count.

Even the sea, in this hour trending
upward the unmeasurable increment
that will have it lapping at our steps
on a November evening, A. D. Twenty Million.

17

Andromeda and fern along the front,
sage and daisies in the backyard's sun.
In the cockeyed, brimming gutter,
salamanders and a seedling tree.
Microclimates: things dig in
exactly where they're supposed to be.

In the brightest window, in the muntin's
sixteenth-inch of shadow, mildew darkens.
Within the shadowy body: deeper shadows,
and shadows within them, favorable enough
that a cell-size shadow repeats and repeats itself.

18

Sparrows raucous in the gutters,
all the contusions of the wind,
sublimation of roof shingles in the moon
will wear a house down.

And nothing destroys a house like confidence.
Understood.
But my anxiety's perfect, I say,
knock-knocking on wood.

19

The raccoon whose custom was to muscle our cans,
was too careless, or too careful, crossing the street,
and lay for a long time upside down,
while whatever was thinking him through slowly concluded
he was reducible to a tooth-white spine.
Like a little drawing of a bridge, I might have added,
and perfectly uncrossed, but whether now
simpler or more difficult I don't know.

20

Bacteria don't know which way is down.
A gnat forgets. Mice fall
unharmed from airliners.
Memo: be small.

21

My daymare is, crossing suspension bridges,
that I'm ordered to build one in the Middle Ages.
I wrack my brains for info about ores,
derive from scratch techniques for smelting,
and analyze the stresses of the catenary.
I have to invent precision tools, but first, precision.
I have to explain, my God, why this is necessary!

22

Someone I can't make out behind the tint
honk-honks. I wave because she thinks I should,
hoping to find out later what I meant.

23

I keep finding in the fur of little tasks
littler tasks,

and in needs, more needs.

How quickly an intuition
becomes a duty,

the faint deer paths
that dirt bikes codify.

24

Antennas waving, button-ended,
where daisies had risen through the slatted seats
of our lawn chairs, a committee in recess,
that I left so carefully in place all summer
as a monument to carelessness.

25

Who frisks me for the hours
I've stolen millions of?
My red alarm says 80:01
or 10:08 (it's upside-down).

26

Disorder chains, but cataclysm frees.
Sighing, I bend for some litter,
but the leaves in crisis, hemispheres of snow
are beyond one man to undo.

27

(Though someone proves that in a dimension *n*
there's a single point
from which these random-seeming, cross-blown leaves
stream out, rays of a sun . . .)

28

Someone is having trouble with the picture,
pixels at the red end wobbling down.
There is shrilling under the dialogue: crickets.
Someone is having trouble with the sound.

From the rained woods, odor of cigar box.
Someone walks through an ember the size of a city.
He suffers uncued tears, the sky's too *sky*.
We apologize for our technical difficulties.

Someone feels like he's walking on a bed
high pillowy and underwater steps,
someone's a wind, he says, with nothing to blow.
Baffling, this glitch in proprioception.

Someone is having trouble with his sequence,
flashback, ellipsis, work-around,
who muffs his big line, *Spare me O death*,
ad-libbing *Come down, whatever, O come down!*

29

In the woods, the soft fall
of the year on the year before.

Deer of evening, browsing, growing bluer.
Who is that at your shoulder but the sun
or someone offering you a mild, gold drink?

30

This midge is a geometer,
driven or deft,
who squares off, eye-level,
turning left and left and left.

Sphere of cabbage whites? Electrons.
Sparrow on glass? A blurted explanation.
The threshing of the deer in leaves
is a child's unwrapping of a package—

and all this accidental happiness,
so simple
that it looks like fate? A sentence
I began at twenty-one with "For example. . . ."

31

And, after all, the guy who admonished us
Don't buy a stick of furniture, or paint
until you have watched four seasons in a house
must have thought all the art in living
was not to live, but to make a place forever.
Perfection's to sell. Happiness, let go:
let the window be a wall, the wall a window.

32

A poor man's cow dies, a rich man's child:
so the archaic proverb goes, unkind
unless the poor man, dreaming that being known
for what he is will bring him all he deserves,
and the rich one, dreading he will be found
to have, already, more than he deserves,
are the same man, rich with loss,
the transparent house within my house,
the empty road that shrills within my roads,
that I cannot live with, cannot live without.

33

Squirrels can circle what we call our lot
at roof-height without ever touching down,
since the trees reach one into another,
shaped deeply by their standing together.

In sharp distinction, solitary trees
approximate their field guide forms,
and poplar is purely poplar or elm elm,
which makes for a half-truth in our human realm:

the soul that blurs in a morning on the phone
grows mirror-clear when I am an hour alone,
sure—but what day, what field's so spacious
that I could unimagine imagination,
and walk out to the middle and be only myself,
not forming your words in my head, not hearing you listen?

34

This evening blue knows everything:
one house and disappearing trees.
It would let me stand for everyone,
but I am tired of its tired anonymous tenderness,
its meaning silence, its universal condescension.

Someone is burning road-chunks against the cold.
someone's pillow is stuffed with maple leaves.
No one can turn his life into another's.
No one can take his riches with him, or his burdens.
Neither rich nor poor shall pass through the eye of the needle.

35

High squirrel against the sun, all haze and blaze,
and loud,
a creature interrupted in its metamorphosis
from tree to cloud.

36

I have seen foot-long fish sailing in the trees
where Millstone rose and left them to blister.

I have seen that the grass is a herd,
slowly turning as the wind turns,

and how dry it is under the roads
and heavy for what lives there.

I have felt in the body fronts and swarms,
now, in autumn, on the move,

and deep in the pool of night the milky blur
of the galaxy's swung arm.

37

Under the sky so huge and restless,
what can we do
but, like the astonished trees,
look up, let go,

all of us tourists at the duty-free,
dropping our last words in the language,
last of our currency.

Now the ripe incapable squirrels
squandered under our tires,
and the slick of leaves,

we drive with swift indifference over the desires
that drove us yesterday,
somehow garish and irrelevant already
as if we were puzzling over them ten years later.

38

Too many years to figure by trial and error
whether it's orange juice or exercise,
the succor of a jay or dumb luck
that saves you, which is the prime hour of the day
for wit or prayer, speed or desire,
or which of your dreams of love go all the way.
No experiment can prove you right or wrong:
too many variables, controls insufficient.
After a time, there's no time for experience.

39

Each instrument of our kitchen,
each handle in my garage
is part of a god who broke up, as gods do,
into aspects—the screwer, the smoother,
the divider into equal streams—
in the storm of prayer reduced to his uses.

Our stories ran out, yes. The story: goes on.
Isn't it art
to find the second use of ourselves, compulsion gone?

40

Now it's just crickets: little
files, drills, hammers.
nothing sadder, lovelier
than their *bleak* and *bleak*,
thinning the fields
the sad heart must have wanted thinner.

41

These are the skies, the waters, kindly metals.
These are the mums, like cliff fires in the mist,
August-fired, jagged happenings
that hardiness has made indelicate.

Now the milkweed rattles and the burdock
harboring the last crickets, counting down,
everywhere late oxides of a beauty
hardly less beautiful as it browns.

The squirrel panics to the curb, the cyclist
hunches, sneaking between the winds,
I drive home wronged, no, wrong—blue twilight
a premature hypothesis.

Day I worked for, just now looking up?
No one mentioned it had come and gone.
Not leaves: it's vision that lets go and blows.
O gravity, divinely video!

And will the mind, mid-winter,
be small as I remember:
noon, the breadth of a windshield;
midnight, lit circle on a letter?

These are the geese, bad oboists,
that one bright gene, vestigial,
remembers how to translate: *all regret*.

Ah Life! But we can live without it.